Raw Conjugate - Foundations

The Complete 'How To' System On Using Conjugate For Raw Powerlifting

Raw Conjugate Series

Book 1

JACOB ROTHENBERG

JACOB ROTHENBERG

Copyright © 2017 Jacob Rothenberg

All rights reserved.

ISBN: 1546925627
ISBN-13: 978-1546925620

The contents of this book may not be reproduced, duplicated or transmitted without direct written permission from the author.

Under no circumstances will any legal responsibility or blame be held against the publisher for any reparation, damages, or monetary loss due to the information herein, either directly or indirectly.

Legal Notice:
This book is copyright protected. This is only for personal use. You cannot amend, distribute, sell, use, quote or paraphrase any part or the content within this book without the consent of the author.

Disclaimer Notice:
Please note the information contained within this document is for educational and entertainment purposes only. Every attempt has been made to provide accurate, up to date and reliable complete information. No warranties of any kind are expressed or implied. Readers acknowledge that the author is not engaging in the rendering of legal, financial, medical or professional advice. The content of this book has been derived from various sources. Please consult a licensed professional before attempting any techniques outlined in this book.

By reading this document, the reader agrees that under no circumstances are is the author responsible for any losses, direct or indirect, which are incurred as a result of the use of information contained within this document, including, but not limited to, —errors, omissions, or inaccuracies.

RAW CONJUGATE - FOUNDATIONS

CONTENTS

1. THE HISTORY OF CONJUGATE – WESTSIDE BARBELL 3
Popularized by Westside 7

2. THE CONJUGATE POWERLIFTING SYSTEM 11

3. RAW vs. GEARED POWERLIFTING 15
Training Differences between Raw Conjugate and Geared Conjugate 17

4. THE MAXIMUM EFFORT METHOD 21
The Method 22
The Max Effort Workout 27

5. THE DYNAMIC EFFORT METHOD 35
The Dynamic Workout 38
Accommodating Resistance 40
The Dynamic Effort Load 41
Accessory Movements for Squats 46
  Dumbbell Step Ups 46
  Rear-Foot Elevated Squat (Also known as the Bulgarian Split Squat) 47
Accessory Movements for the Bench Press 48
  Lying Barbell Tricep Extension 48

Close-Grip Bench Press (Flat or Inclined)...........49
Bent-Over Barbell Row...49
Banded Tricep Pushdowns 50
Accessory Movements for the Deadlift..............51
Kettlebell Swings..51
The Lower-Trap Raise..52
Bridge (Hip Thrusts) – Barbell Version 53

6. FINE TUNING CONJUGATE FOR RAW LIFTING..55

8. PUTTING IT TOGETHER 67

Monday (Max Effort Lower) 67
Wednesday (Max Effort Upper) 68
Friday (Dynamic Effort Lower)...............................69
Saturday (Dynamic Effort Upper) 70
General Guidelines 71

CONCLUSION 75

ABOUT THE AUTHOR..79

RAW CONJUGATE - FOUNDATIONS

INTRODUCTION

I have been lifting weights for 15 years and have been competing in powerlifting for the last 8 of those years.

Having started with weight training when I was 14, my story is not typical of how most kids get into lifting. Some kids start going to the weight room as part of their training for a school sport.

Some kids lift weights in order to get bigger and try to impress girls on their high school campus.

Me?

I never attended high school. Or even middle school, for that matter.

Growing up as a young kid, I always had a knack for academics. I was an extremely fast learner, and thrived in a classroom setting.

On nationwide standardized tests, I would rank in the 99th percentile in math and had the writing ability of a 9th grader when I was 8 years old.

My label going through the years of elementary school was as a child prodigy, and soon after finishing the 5th grade & being bored to tears with the standard public school curriculum, I found myself transferring to a community college at 11 years old.

While being Jimmy Neutron on campus was very fun for the first couple years, I found myself being socially isolated to some degree with the rest of my classmates. How can you be a child genius with lots of college friends when you can't even drive?

While I was happy throughout my time in community college, I wanted to have bit of a more normal social life and try to fit in better.

So, when I transferred to UC Davis when I was 14 to finish my Bachelors degree, I figured – why not start lifting weights to put on some muscle and look more like an incoming freshman?

If there was a poster boy for being so called "hard gainer", it was me. Standing at 5'10 and 128 pounds soaking wet, I had a lot of work ahead of me.

Starting out at the gym, I couldn't even press an empty bar and had to start out pressing the 15 lb. dumbbells.

Through the magic powers of newbie gains and

researching how to train & eat better from Bodybuilding.com, I saw initial success and was able to bulk up by 20 pounds in a year.

When I was able to put on some muscle, I achieved my goal of looking slightly older in appearance and I was able to have a social circle on campus where less people asked about my age.

Having done this though, I had a realization in the gym – I actually enjoyed lifting weights, and more so: I kept track of how much weight I could do on movements, always wanting to lift more.

After learning about the 3 lift sport of powerlifting and seeing that it was *all* about how much weight one could perform, I took a casual interest in powerlifting.

After having graduated from UC Davis and immediately starting in the working world, I stayed active with lifting weights but didn't pursue powerlifting as a sport to compete in until I was 21 years old.

From the time I started lifting in the gym, it took me 7 years of training to bench 225 pounds for a max. I had good genetics in the book smarts department…and not so much with possessing natural strength.

Still, I mustered up the courage to do my first powerlifting meet at a gym called Diablo Barbell.

As one could expect during a first time experience at a powerlifting meet, the whole thing was so surreal to me.

Lifters were squatting in excess of 800 pounds, a teenage

girl benched 315 and I saw one of Diablo Barbell's best lifters at the time deadlift 585 as a warm-up.

These were some strong people, with strength beyond my imagination! Meanwhile, I managed to squeak by with a 1,025 pound raw total at 198 pounds – but no one made fun of me for my first time total.

Instead, the same community of strong lifters congratulated me on a good job and encouraged me to continue getting stronger & keep competing. I was hooked.

Since taking up powerlifting as a competitive hobby up until today, my training routine has been based on the Conjugate System.

Like most people starting out in an area where everyone was lifting "Westside", I scraped up what information I could from studying Louie Simmons' articles and by reading up what I could on internet forums about the methodology.

I eventually joined my first powerlifting team for a gym called Wild Iron in San Jose, where I was able to refine my understanding of "Westside Conjugate" a little bit better.

That being said, there was one issue that always stuck out with me while training using the team's system – I was a raw lifter, and not all of what we were doing training-wise seemed to make logical sense with regards to carryover for the raw lifts.

Despite this, I made great progress with overall strength

and eventually totaled 1,515 pounds raw at 242 in 2013 as a Wild Iron team member.

I was becoming stronger from the virtue of training in a powerlifting gym with a great coach, but as I improved I started noticing flaws with how I was progressing.

I was getting injured with muscle strains every few months, and I'd have a competition lift that stalled for 5-6 months at a time with no progress – even while training hard and not slacking off.

And even though I was improving, my progress was not THAT great – it had taken me 3 years to progress from a 315 pound bench to pressing 369 pounds in competition.

In the big picture of things given my novice background, this was slow progress and I could do better. Last – I just could not put on muscle mass past a certain point.

I was walking around at 235 pounds and looked like I lifted weights, but I wasn't jacked and juicy like the better lifters looked. Something seemed off, and something had to change.

By the end of my tenure in Wild Iron, I was starting to have disagreements with teammates on how to train.

I realized that excess accommodating resistance (bands & chains) were unnecessary for a raw lifter, but for some reason some of the other guys wanted to squat with 200 pounds of tension on speed day – without being able to squat 405 pounds raw.

Likewise, when I made the conclusion that my quadriceps

were my sticking point at raw squatting & that I should incorporate more leg work, no one took me seriously because Westside's "template" training system never included quad work.

Due to some burnout with no longer enjoying training, I walked away from the team and left powerlifting for a year and a half.

In 2015, I decided to return to powerlifting and change things up by training under the tutelage of Jesse Burdick. I had known of Jesse through his association with Mark Bell and from his reputation for being one of the premier coaches in powerlifting.

Upon joining his powerlifting team, I found that Jesse did all the programming for the team using Conjugate – but unlike the typical "Westside style" cookie cutter programs I had encountered prior, Jesse's system was completely different.

There was a ton more volume overall, the choice in accessory movements were a bit unorthodox with step-ups being an occasional accessory exercise, and max effort training did not always translate to lifting for a max single.

While I was a bit skeptical of all the changes at first, I eventually followed Jesse's full program after a couple weeks of getting used to the higher volume.

Fast forward to now - I have been working with Jesse Burdick as my coach for the past 2 years and have made incredible progress.

In March 2016, I totaled 1,466 pounds at 220 at his meet.

At Reebok Record Breakers 2 in November of the same year, I ended up totaling 1,686 at 242.

That's 220 lbs. on my total in only 8 months! And let me tell you, it is hell of a lot harder to take a 1,466 total to 1,686 than it is from 1,025 to 1,225 in 8 months (which would still be impressive regardless).

While a lot of things came into play with the big increase onto my total (such as the jump up in weight class), the culmination of Jesse's innovations to the Conjugate System made all the difference.

I truly believe that Jesse Burdick is the current foremost expert in utilizing the Conjugate System for raw lifters, and the proof shows with his athletes' results.

Tiffany Leung is the current 97 lb. world record holder in the squat, having performed a 292 pound squat at Record Breakers 2.

Jeremy Avila is an upcoming powerlifter with a world class total of 2,000 pounds raw at 220, and he continues to improve at a fast rate.

Even Cailer Woolam, the first man to ever deadlift 400 kilograms at 90 kilograms bodyweight has sought Jesse for long distance coaching in prospects of becoming one of the greatest lifters of all time.

In addition to these accolades, Jesse has taken many other lifters to reaching an elite classification and achieving their best numbers on the platform.

I am one of those lifters, and I will share with you the current iteration of the Conjugate System for raw lifting as how I've learned it from Jesse, while also learning how it should not be from past experience.

To state the obvious, I am not taking credit for Jesse's contributions to Conjugate, nor am I claiming that I've invented anything. I would simply like to make my contribution to the sport of powerlifting by documenting everything I've learned and sharing it with the open masses.

Thank you for buying *Raw Conjugate – Foundations*!

This is the first title of a four book series to cover the Conjugate System.

"*Foundations*" sets the general methodology in place for using Conjugate as a raw lifter.

The next three books to be released will cover each of the competitive lifts in substantial detail on how to train them under the umbrella of Conjugate.

I hope my work is found of value to you and that you further improve as a powerlifter while you are on the road to reaching your personal success within the sport.

JACOB ROTHENBERG

1. THE HISTORY OF CONJUGATE – WESTSIDE BARBELL

"If I wanted to continue to make progress, I had to get stronger and I had to get smarter. Much smarter."
Louie Simmons

Back in 1980, a man now synonymous with some of the strongest and most elite powerlifters of all time was beginning to build a superior strength training system that would one day become renowned worldwide.

His name is Louie Simmons, also known as the founder of the Westside Barbell and "godfather" of the Conjugate Method as it has been most popularly understood in the United States.

With more than 50 years of experience on and off the

platform, competing in dozens - and coaching in hundreds - of meets, Louie himself is 1 of only 5 powerlifters in history to total Elite in 5 different weight classes.

He has totaled Elite continuously from February 1973 to December 2009 – his last Elite total being at 62 years old.

He has been a top 10 lifter for 30 years and ranked 4th nationally in 2000.

To be able to squat 920, bench press 600, and deadlift 722 pounds at any age is incredible. Yet, Louie is the only person over 50 years old to have done so.

These numbers are however, not rare for those who trained with Louie at Westside Barbell.

With 23 athletes deadlifting over 800 pounds and 3 who deadlift over 900 pounds, Westside Barbell also boasts 15 members who have a totals over 2,500 pounds and 7 with an over 2,600 pound total.

It's pretty safe to say that Louie is a master at what he does – and not solely based on what he personally has achieved as a powerlifter within the sport.

In this current era of powerlifting, he is known for a legacy of creating world class competitors on a level nothing short of phenomenal.

Not only being adept at achieving feats of strength on his own behalf, Louie has the talent and knowledge to create world champions that will be remembered in the sport forever.

As testimony to Louie's claim that the conjugate method could be applied to a broad demographic of athletes, he has shown his versatility of the Westside Conjugate philosophy by training athletes in other sports.

It was common for NFL teams to seek consulting from Louie, along with various champions & world class athletes from other sports who are often mentioned in his own articles.

There is no doubt that the conjugate method of powerlifting designed by Louie Simmons is extremely effective in developing maximal strength for the squat, bench and deadlift respectively, making his unique methodology a revolutionary force in the realm of powerlifting.

In nearly every powerlifting gym, there is a presence of bands, chains, and boards.

Though these can all be used independently of the conjugate method, and the conjugate method can be run WITHOUT the use of any of these – it is undeniable that Westside's influence to powerlifting is greatly profound.

It's not surprising though that Louie's Westside methods were developed over the course of 40 or so years with origins back in the 1960s.

When shuttles were being launched into space the Soviets, and the Bulgarians were already miles ahead in terms of their training for strength, evident in the success of their Olympic weightlifters.

Having competed in his first powerlifting meet in 1966 and having served in the Army for five years afterwards, Louie found himself training at the original Westside Barbell gym in Culver City, California.

At this gym, he met and trained with four future world champions who would help change the course of history for strength training, and teach Louie the fundamentals of the conjugate method.

These principles would later be developed into what is known today as the Westside Method.

Those four world powerlifting champions were Milt McKinney, George Crawford, Larry Pacifico, and Vince Anello.

Looking at their methods of training - each with their own unique strengths, Simmons noticed it was the addition of accessory movements that helped them to gain strength and find great success in the 3 competition lifts.

For example:

- George's training was a combination of a number of different squat variations – box squatting being one of those. He was also known for the use of good mornings in his training.

- Larry Pacifico had an incredible bench due to lots of triceps work in combination with high volume bodybuilding training.

- When asked by Louie Simmons about what

helped with his deadlift, Vince Anello replied "everything helps my deadlift". Being that Vince was the first man to ever deadlift 800 while under 200 pounds, Louie apparently took his advice to heart.

Alongside these incredible lifters, and many others in the 1960s and 70s, the conjugate system that eventually popularized and synonymous with Westside Barbell was born.

> *"Louie didn't invent the Conjugate System. He just made it better." - Dave Tate*

Popularized by Westside

Westside Barbell in Columbus, Ohio is an invite only powerlifting club solely led by Louie Simmons.

Not only have the thousands of hours been clocked up whilst perfecting the Westside system - it is the culmination of blood, sweat and tears from lifters who have come in seeking their pursuit of greatness while ultimately bowing out of the sport competitively for each of their own personal reasons.

It is the result of a multi-decade love affair with powerlifting at the most elite level of competition, along with countless hours of pain, experimentation and hard work.

Simmons is a lifelong student of human development. Westside truly is his Magnum Opus.

Though the conjugate system was originally used in the 60s, there is some ambiguity as to who actually invented it.

Per the information given on Westside Barbell's website - in 1964, Dr. Yuri Verkhoshansky was credited through his publications for what we know today as the conjugate system.

That being said, a Bulgarian coach by the name of Abadjieve, had a similar plan for waving volume and intensities (sometimes referred to as the Pendulum Wave), which is a key component of the conjugate system.

Having studied meticulously the hundreds of journals and data developed by the greatest of the Russian and Bulgarian weightlifters, Simmons has taken the best of the methods devised by the Soviets and the Bulgarians and put them into one system - the famous Westside Barbell Conjugate System.

Essentially, the Westside style conjugate system is the collaboration of two advanced training systems:

1. The Bulgarian system, which has the trainee using near-max lifts every workout, and

2. The Soviet system, which has several special exercises that are used by superior lifters and athletes, to advance their training.

With a main goal to "become the best and push every boundary known to man in doing so", the Westside system has resulted in numerous records being broken as well as an impressive list of other achievements in multi-ply powerlifting:

- With 2 over 2700 pound totals, 5 over 2800 pounds and Dave Hoff who has 3,005 lbs – the biggest multi-ply total of all time.

- One athlete holds the current Westside Barbell gym record of a 63.5 inch box jump.

- There are 36 men who've benched more than 700 pounds, with two athletes having benched 900.

- Out of the 19 athletes that have squatted 1000 pounds in competition, 2 have squatted have squatted 1,200. If that is not strong, nothing in this world is.

JACOB ROTHENBERG

2. THE CONJUGATE POWERLIFTING SYSTEM

When it comes to powerlifting, the right strength training system can distinguish the difference between winning and losing, staying healthy and getting injured..

One of the best ways to train in order to get stronger and lift heavier is the concept of periodization.

Simply put, periodization refers to dividing your strength training program into separate training sequences or blocks, each focusing on a specific set of athletic qualities.

As a powerlifter, periodization will help you lift heavier and heavier weights.

Periodization can be classified into several types.

But in this book, we'll focus on just one system that has a

proven track record of making elite powerlifters out of average ones – the Conjugate Periodization system.

Conjugate Periodization is a system that makes use of different training techniques with the objective of improving a powerlifter's important athletic qualities simultaneously.

These qualities include among others: absolute strength, explosiveness, agility, and speed.

Louie Simmons, developed what is probably the most popular version of the Conjugate system in the United States, which is the Westside Barbell method.

The Westside Barbell Method (WBM) works by combining 3 basic strength-training methods.

These methods are:

1. The Maximal Effort Method
2. The Dynamic Effort Method
3. The Repetition Method

The Maximal Effort Method (also referred to as Max Effort) involves lifting a maximum weight for a 1 rep max, which is used by powerlifters to achieve the biggest gains in strength and power.

The Dynamic Effort Method requires lifting submaximal weight as fast as possible with an increased amount of overall volume compared to the Max Effort session.

The Repetition Method requires lifting submaximal weight

until muscular failure, and this is typically employed to produce more optimal gains in hypertrophy / muscle mass.

The Westside Barbell Method utilizes a relatively short training cycle, or microcycle that lasts for 7 days. Within each cycle, the intensity and volume of training is adjusted depending on the scheduled method for the day.

This cycle or pattern is based on such changes in intensity and volume during the week, i.e., the higher the volume (reps and sets), the lower the intensity (weight of the lift), and vice versa.

By cycling one's training methods within each cycle, powerlifters can train and progress in all necessary strength qualities needed for powerlifting at the same time.

It is this simultaneous training of the necessary strength qualities that sets Conjugate Periodization apart from all other strength training methods which utilize a more traditional form of periodization that dedicates mesocycles (2-8 week long training weeks) to quality one at a time.

JACOB ROTHENBERG

3. RAW vs. GEARED POWERLIFTING

Before we go on to the meat of the Conjugate system, I want to distinguish between 2 types of powerlifters: "raw" and "geared" lifters.

The key difference – the demarcation line so to speak – that distinguishes one from the other is the use of equipment that leverages a powerlifter's strength and power, allowing to lift more weight than what he/she normally could without such equipment.

It has been estimated that using powerlifting gear can increase a powerlifter's lift anywhere from 5% to even 20% more than their current raw maximum.

For those who are already quite adept at using such gear, the increase can be substantially higher.

But still, the fine line that separates "raw" powerlifters from geared ones continues to be very, very fine given that, as of now, there isn't a consistent, universal set of rules or standards that distinguish raw lifting from geared lifting in all current powerlifting federations.

The only consistent standard for classifying lifting competitions as raw in most federations is the use of approved singlets, lifting belts, knee sleeves, wrist wraps and chalk only.

Some federations will promote a "classic raw" division, where knee wraps can be utilized and have infinitely much more added carryover to an individual's squat than knee sleeves ever can.

Consequently, geared or equipped lifting competitions are those that allow powerlifters to use equipment that is not allowed in "raw" events.

Such equipment isn't just meant for protection but as mentioned earlier, allow powerlifters to lift heavier weight than what they can normally perform on their own or with minimal equipment.

Some of the gear or equipment used in geared or equipped powerlifting events include deadlift suits, bench press shirts, and squat suits.

Training Differences between Raw Conjugate and Geared Conjugate

One of the areas where raw and geared conjugate training differs is range of motion or movements.

Geared powerlifters have the advantage of simply focusing on developing strength on the top end of every lift or the range of motion because their gear helps or assists them at the bottom portion, which is the most difficult range of motion for the majority of raw lifters.

Because raw powerlifters don't have the benefit of using gear or equipment that makes it easier to move through the bottom range of motion of every lift, they need to give significantly more attention to strengthening the concerned muscles all throughout their full range of motion during lifts.

In other words, raw conjugate training requires training with a full range of motion (ROM) much more than with geared conjugate lifting.

Another area of difference between the raw and geared conjugate training methods is the practicing of lifts that will be performed in competitions, or the requirement of utilizing specificity into the training program.

Compared to their geared counterparts, raw conjugate lifters utilize significantly less movements in training.

As such, raw powerlifters use a lesser pool of exercises & variations when using the max effort method.

This necessitates the need to perform competition lifts, i.e., deadlifts, squats, and bench presses, more closely compared to geared powerlifters which almost exclusively utilize box squats, board presses, and so forth during a training cycle.

Volume of training is another key difference between raw conjugate and geared conjugate training.

Because raw powerlifters have minimal equipment support, they aren't able to lift as much poundage as their geared brethren.

In order to make up for the difference in poundage, raw powerlifters tend to do more, i.e., perform more volume (total reps x sets) than their geared counterpart.

Lastly, raw conjugate powerlifting has a more even balance of performing squats and deadlifts in training, while geared conjugate powerlifting is geared more towards squats on Dynamic Effort days.

I would theorize that because powerlifting gear or equipment may be more useful for squats than the deadlift, there is more of a needed to prioritize squat training for the biggest total possible.

That being said, there are also plenty of geared lifters who possess great deadlifts regardless of whether they decide to use a suit or not.

Still – while there are world class powerlifters who pull over 800 pounds in spite of not pulling very often in training, **you** likely need to deadlift more often.

World class powerlifters have their deadlift setup memorized in their sleep; you and I need to deadlift at least once a week for a decent amount of sets in order to hone proper setup & technique.

Practice is key while you're still learning!

JACOB ROTHENBERG

4. THE MAXIMUM EFFORT METHOD

Many people consider the maximum effort – or max effort – method to be the most effective of the three Conjugate training methods for building strength. Why?

It's because of its ability to help improve coordination between and within muscles used for powerlifting, as the human body tends to adapt only to the particular stimulus applied to it.

The greatest gains in power and strength are achieved using this method.

That's why despite the fact that some powerlifters who use this method may from time to time experience hypertension, fatigue, anxiety, and even injuries, it continues to be considered the best and most well known method among the three.

Because of the sheer intensity and weight load involved with the max effort method, it should only be used with compound exercises, i.e., multi-joint ones that involve multiple muscle groups.

Max Effort is almost exclusively reserved for deadlifts, bench presses, and squats. Do not use max effort on isolation or single joint exercises such as arm curls, leg curls, or side laterals as too much load on small and isolated muscles will put you at high risk for injuries.

The Method

The max effort method traditionally requires that you work with weights up to your 1 repetition max, or 1-rep max for the day.

In the modern version of conjugate training as we are

seeing it evolve for raw powerlifters, **max effort day does not require you lift to a max single for your primary movement.**

Along with programming max singles for Max Effort, you will also need training weeks where you are reaching for a max triple or even max set of 5 reps as your top set.

I will explain in greater detail as to why this is now being done in the conjugate system in a later section of this book.

As a recommendation for warming up on this day, you should do perform 10% increments leading up to around 80% of your projected for the day, which will start your main working sets.

The repetitions that you'll need to perform won't all be done in one set but in multiple, spread out intervals.

As you advance, i.e., lift more weight, the less reps you perform.

So how can you know your 1-rep max weight for a specific

lift?

There are 2 ways to go about it. One is by far the most simple and accurate way – just go to the weight and lift to see what your max is.

But that can be risky if you're training at a commercial gym and don't have established maxes for movements.

Hence, I will show a 2nd way of estimating your 1-rep max.

A less accurate, but safer way of estimating it would be through the use of mathematical formulas that online rep calculators have used.

Yes, this is not how you should determine your 1 rep max but if you're truly starting out from scratch and don't have a team to work with, you can use this method as a baseline.

But before you can use the formulas, you'll first need to do some lifting and figure out the maximum weight you can lift for 4 to 6 reps for a specific lift.

Once you figured out your 4 to 6 rep max (4-6 max) for a

specific lift, use an online one rep max calculator to have a **rough** idea of what your 1 rep max is.

Estimates are worth nothing until validated or tested. Because the max effort workout's based primarily on your 1-rep max, it's crucial that you're able to validate your estimates and if needed, adjust it accordingly.

When validating your 1-rep max, don't be all gung-ho and go at it alone.

Remember, you'll be handling extremely heavy weight (relative to your own strength, of course) and if you don't have strong and capable spotters to help you out, your risks for an accident or a serious injury are very high.

Remember, the most important thing is your safety, not a 1-rep max that risks injury for you.

So, how do you go about training to your 1-rep max for a given session?

You'll have to do it gradually through a proper warm up.

And here's how you do it.

First, get your whole body warmed up and the blood flowing by riding a stationary bike, dragging a sled on your parking lot pavement, or by going through your usual mobility routine.

When you're done, lift progressively heavier weights on your specific lift leading up to your 1-rep max attempt, roughly in this scheme:

- 50% of 1 rep max for 5 reps;
- 60% of 1 rep max for 3 reps;
- 70% of 1 rep max for 2-3 reps;
- 80% of 1 rep max for 1 rep;
- 90% of 1 rep max for 1 rep; and
- Keep performing singles until you reach your 1 rep max for the day

Pay very close attention to how you feel, especially during the last 2 sets. Adjust accordingly if the lift feels either too light or too heavy.

When attempting your 1-rep max, it's important that you

focus on the lift and put all your attention towards setting up properly and getting tight before performing the lift.

You must always be cognizant of keeping proper form because a mistake in technique puts you at greater risk of getting injured.

The Max Effort Workout

Your max effort workouts should be made up of the primary or main powerlifting exercises, i.e., squats, bench, and deadlifts.

The key to not burning out from lifting a max load every week is to rotate the exercises being used for a given movement weekly.

For example – if you were to perform a bench press against bands last week, you could opt to perform a full range bench press using a Buffalo Bar (a specialty bar that allows for greater range of motion than a standard barbell).

Another crucial aspect of the raw conjugate system is to get a sufficient amount of volume performed for

every Max Effort day.

While the overall volume will still pale in comparison to your Dynamic Effort workouts, you need to be pushing it a little hard overall with the volume done during Max Effort.

The most simple and effective way to achieve this is by performing 1-2 drop sets after your top weight, for as many reps as possible (AMRAP).

As a general guideline, you can drop set off 70-80% of a max you've hit in a workout for 1-2 sets.

For example, if you squat a max triple of 405 pounds for a prescribed training session, you can drop set to 70% of 405 and perform 285 pounds for 2 AMRAP sets.

This is necessary to achieve the overall amount of volume needed to progress as a raw lifter – don't skimp out on AMRAP sets!

Followed after your primary movement, **you usually want to incorporate a second barbell movement as your**

"secondary" exercise.

This will still involve a variation of a barbell lift, but with a utilization of a higher rep scheme (5-20 reps in general) that will cause less toll on you physically, but still cause a significant amount of muscular fatigue necessary for strength and hypertrophy.

This would ideally be geared towards your weak points; if you have assessed that you have weak quadriceps for example, you can incorporate light pause squats of 40-50% from your 1 rep max for sets of high reps.

The exception to performing a second barbell movement is if you've had to perform a max deadlift movement that is either very close within specificity of the competition lift, or if you have been murdered by the sheer stress that your max effort pull induced on your back.

In this case, most lifters are not in a state where they can efficiently perform squat repetitions with good form and you could instead opt straight to accessory movements.

Accessory exercises, which are designed to help you

strengthen the weak areas or muscles used in performing the key powerlifting movements, consist of your remaining training session.

Just as how during your max effort workouts, priority is placed on doing the base powerlifting movements first, accessory training is done at the latter part of the workout.

This ensures that bulk of your energy is expended on what matters the most, which is being able to perform your primary movement (on either Max Effort or Dynamic Day).

One of the major guidelines for max effort workouts under the conjugate system is to use many sets (8 to 12 per workout) for the main lift with very few reps per set (1-5). Even if you wanted to skip this guideline, you won't be able to because lifting close to your 1-rep max for up to 12 sets per session is so intense that it can make you puke!

Another major guideline to observe is gradual progression. This means you don't just go straight to your main sets, which is 85% to 90% of your 1-rep max.

That'd be suicide as going from zero to that much weight puts you at high risk for muscle tears.

Be smart and take the time to accumulate some volume through your warm-ups. This means starting with an empty bar, loading up with 135 (or even 95 pounds if necessary), then working up with 3 reps per set and gradually increase in weight until you get to your main sets, wherein you'll be lifting to a prescribed rep max.

Keep in mind that for optimal gains in strength while trying to avoid injury, don't try to perform more than 6-7 singles at 90% or more of your 1-rep max every weekly workout. Aim for a sweet spot of 3-5 solid singles after you've made it past warm-ups to a 90% intensity range.

Past that, you are somewhat compromising the ability to progress in poundage as you will inevitably fatigue through the series of sets.

You want to stay relatively fresh while being able to hit the highest weight possible for a given workout.

Rest and recuperation is another key ingredient to making

steady gains in strength and power.

Perform max effort workouts after at least 72 hours from your last dynamic effort one to ensure your body is able to fully recover and recharge for the grueling workout that is the max effort method.

And during workouts, your rest in between sets can take as long as you want because the point here is that you have enough on your gas tank to eke out the next set with heavy poundage.

Just be somewhat reasonable and not take 20 minutes between sets – if this is a problem for you, get in better shape!

RAW CONJUGATE - FOUNDATIONS

JACOB ROTHENBERG

5. THE DYNAMIC EFFORT METHOD

As mentioned previously, the Dynamic Effort Method is a method that requires lifting a submaximal weight as fast as possible.

Why such a requirement?

It's because for optimal powerlifting, you'll need more than just strength – you'll also need speed and power, both of which can be developed through this type of training.

To put it in layman's terms, Dynamic Effort training is one that's designed to optimize acceleration or speed of sub-maximal loads (weights).

And when we talk about sub-maximal loads, we're referring to using weights that are significantly less than your 1-rep max.

So why do you need speed and power to work alongside strength?

How does it help you lift more weight as you do when powerlifting?

You see, when you exert maximum force to lift something for a certain number of repetitions, you improve your body's motor unit recruitment efficiency.

As such, you generate maximum force to lift or move heavy weights in the gym when you do singles, doubles, or triples, which in turn improves your body's motor recruitment efficiency.

However, it's not possible to lift heavy weights for extended periods of time due to your body's limited capacity for recovering from such a very strenuous workload.

If you insist in continuing to work out with such heavy poundage, you'll eventually get injured. For the vast majority of lifters, a training day calling for lighter loads of weight to be lifted is necessary to balance out the Max Effort method.

And this is where dynamic effort workouts come into play.

You can further improve or optimize your motor recruitment efficiency without having to sustain very heavy lifting for extended periods of time.

You can also do that in between max effort workouts, i.e.,

recovery periods, by lifting substantially less weight at a much faster and explosive pace.

But why all the fuss about improving motor unit efficiency?

Think about driving a Lamborghini sports car in a busy metropolis.

Because the streets are relatively narrow with high vehicular density, i.e., large number of vehicles on the road per unit of area, you can't maximize all that horsepower beneath the hood.

You may not even be able to go faster than 20 miles per hour!

When you get on the freeway such as Germany's Autobahn however, things will drastically change.

From a bumper-to-bumper traffic situation, you're now in a much, much wider road with significantly less vehicular density, where the minimum average speed is 45 miles per hour!

In a freeway (assuming there's no vehicular accident that's causing a massive traffic jam), you can put your car's pedal to the metal and optimize all that horsepower underneath the hood.

Because of the wider road and less cars, you can go as fast as your car can possibly can.

There's practically no hindrance to optimal recruitment of your car engine's power.

It's the same with your muscles.

The more efficient your body becomes at recruiting motor units or muscles when exerting effort, the more weight it can lift!

It's like widening the road on which you drive a sports car, which gives it the opportunity to go really, really fast.

The Dynamic Workout

Because the emphasis of the dynamic workout is speed and power, you will use only 50% to 70% of your 1-rep max, compared to working towards a maximum weight under the max effort workout.

This means if you're able to deadlift 300 pounds for a 1-rep max, you'll only be working with at most 225 pounds.

Because of the significant drop in the amount of weight you'll be handling in this type of workout, **the true purpose of this day is to put in the volume necessary to make strength gains in your lifts**.

While most novice and intermediate powerlifters can understand the premise of improving motor unit efficiency, they overlook the necessity to put out a significant amount of volume on DE day when having done significantly less volume on Max Effort Day.

Also, you'll need to perform your reps much faster to compensate for the big reduction in the weight you'll be lifting.

And finally, the substantial reduction in weight and effort per set or rep means you won't be quite as fatigued from each set.

Ideally, your rest period in between sets should be minimal – between 30 to 60 seconds only.

What the dynamic effort lacks in weight or resistance it makes up for with total volume, i.e. more total reps due to more sets.

If you think it's easy or a walk in the park, it really isn't.

You may be using substantially less weight but aside from higher volume, you will also be performing the lifting movements in a very fast and explosive manner.

And those are enough to ensure you still work out your key muscles optimally in order to lift progressively heavier weights.

As with the max effort workout, you will need to let at least 72 hours pass from your last workout, be it dynamic or max effort, before performing the workout again.

This ensures your body's better recovered and able to take on the next workload.

Accommodating Resistance

Accommodating resistance refers to additional resistance applied to specific lifts, particularly when doing dynamic effort workouts.

It's what you see when a powerlifter uses chains or elastic bands – attached to the barbell – prior to performing lifts.

When bands or chains are attached to the barbell, it increases the resistance particularly at the tail end of a lift's concentric or positive phase.

Why do powerlifters who perform dynamic workouts employ accommodating resistance using chains or bands?

Don't dynamic workouts need to use substantially less weight in order to improve one's speed and power when it comes to lifting?

If that's the case, why do you still need additional resistance? Why not just add more weight?

The reason for this is resistance or tension throughout a lift's full range of motion, which is of prime importance for raw lifters as compared to geared ones, isn't constant.

Specifically, leverage is greatest at the tail end of a lift's concentric or positive phase, i.e., resistance is least. Using chains and bands for adding accommodating resistance allows you to add extra resistance just at that point where resistance is weakest.

Because it only adds resistance on towards the latter part

of a lift's concentric movement, it has the effect of "smoothing out" the amount of resistance you're subjected to all throughout your lift's full range of motion.

Another reason why powerlifters use accommodating resistance is to strengthen weak points. For example, if a bench presser's triceps aren't as strong as his chest, he'll have a difficult time with his press later on.

Using bands and chains for promoting accommodating resistance can help him address his weak triceps during benches.

Lastly, the most significant benefit of accommodating resistance is the ability to improve lifting power quickly.

Because using accommodating resistance requires a lifter to continuously perform lifting movements at substantially faster speeds, he or she can more quickly develop or increase their lifting power.

The Dynamic Effort Load

As mentioned earlier, the dynamic effort method uses significantly less weight, i.e., only 50% to 70% of your 1-rep max.

However, you'll be adding extra or accommodating resistance to some of your sessions via resistance bands or chains in order to maintain relatively constant resistance or tension, especially at the latter part of your lift's concentric or positive phase.

Here's a good example of how the dynamic effort load looks like for the squat:

- **Weight** – 205 & 245 lbs
- **Accommodating Resistance** – 80 lbs of chain
- **Repetitions** = 3 reps
- **Sets** = 5 sets with 205 lbs, followed by 5 sets with 245 lbs
- **Total Lifts** = 30
- **Total Weight Volume** = 6,750 lbs + chain weight

It is worth noting that contrast does NOT have to be used often for dynamic effort workouts on ANY of the lifts, contrary to popular belief.

Just as how it does not make sense for a lifter who is stuck off their chest in benching to be overemphasizing board presses in their routine, accommodating resistance should not be the "bread and butter" of the weights you lift – regular weight should be when your sticking point is at the bottom of the lift.

For your dynamic effort lower day, ALWAYS include deadlifting as part of your routine along with squats; squats are to be performed first, then deadlifts are done thereafter. As mentioned earlier in the "Raw Conjugate vs. Geared Conjugate" section of this book, it is absolutely necessary to work on your deadlift by *actually deadlifting* as opposed to solely relying on special exercises to build up strength that will carry over to your deadlift.

Unless you are a deadlift prodigy freak, you need to be practicing the technique of your pull at least once a week and work on mastering your form throughout your training years.

JACOB ROTHENBERG

6. GENERAL ACCESSORY MOVEMENTS

While your workouts are primarily all about being able to develop power, speed and strength to perform major lifts, it's not enough to just perform the base or main movements.

Why?

Considering that the base movements are compound, i.e., involves multiple muscle groups and joints, there's bound to be a weak link that can prevent you from making significant progress or worse, get you injured.

Hence, the need for accessory movements!

These are exercises that are performed specifically to develop those reinforcing muscles needed for hoisting very heavy weight when performing the base movements.

This may well be one of the most important aspects of the

raw conjugate system, because it allows you to custom fit your training program to the extent that you can strengthen your weak spots.

Below is a short playbook of just some of the accessories you can use for each of your lifting days.

Most of the exercises listed are actually used in our iteration of the conjugate system. We have these exercises programmed in our training sessions, and you should rotate them in from time to time.

No exercise is "below you" if it serves a valid purpose in your training.

If you are too much of an alpha male to perform dumbbell step ups, you can stay stuck in the past about "old school training" and achieve results that are non-optimal at best.

Keep an open mind when incorporating new accessory movements and add it to your repertoire if you can reap benefits from using it.

Accessory Movements for Squats

Dumbbell Step Ups

This is a good exercise that can help you improve your range of motion on the squats (important for raw lifters), strengthen your connective tissues, and strengthen the quad muscles, all of which affect the surrounding area around your knees.

Here's how to perform the exercise:

> Working on the right leg first, stand beside a step up platform with your right foot on the platform and your left foot flat on the floor.
>
> Push yourself up with your right leg – elevating your left leg and feet off the floor – and at the top of the movement, let your left foot make contact with the platform.
>
> Return to the starting position in a controlled manner, where your right foot is once again still on the platform. Perform 3 to 4 sets of 10 to 15 reps with weights, using dumbbells on both hands.
>
> Do the same for the left leg immediately after completion of your set, switching positions thereafter.

Rear-Foot Elevated Squat (Also known as the Bulgarian Split Squat)

This workout helps you further strengthen your adductor muscles as well your legs for lifting heavier weights.

To perform:

> With a barbell over your shoulders or a pair of

dumbbells in hand, stand in front of a bench with the right foot resting on it.

Perform 10 to 20 squats using only your left leg, keeping yourself well balanced.

Switch legs and do the same.

Perform 3 to 4 sets per leg.

Accessory Movements for the Bench Press

Lying Barbell Tricep Extension

Along with the shoulders and chest, the most crucial muscles for optimal raw bench pressing are your triceps.

This exercise lets you strengthen the long heads of your triceps, which most other triceps isolation exercises aren't able to work out optimally.

To perform this exercise:

Lie down on a bench and hold a barbell up as if you'll be performing a set of close-gripped bench presses.

While keeping your arms perpendicular to your chest, i.e., at a 90-degree angle, lower the barbell as close to your head as possible, bending at the elbows only.

Return to starting position. Do 2 to 4 sets of 8 to 12

reps each.

If using a barbell aggravates your elbow joints or an existing case of elbow tendonitis, you can try mitigating the pain by switching to dumbbells instead.

Close-Grip Bench Press (Flat or Inclined)

If you're having trouble at the lockout part of your press, this will help strengthen your triceps to address that weakness while still giving you a full range of motion for pressing.

Perform a regular bench or incline press, with the only difference being your grip, i.e., your hands are positioned 8 to 12 inches apart.

Perform 3 to 5 sets of 10 to 15 reps each.

This can also be performed with a heavier, low rep weight scheme when interchanged as a secondary barbell movement for your Max Effort bench day.

Bent-Over Barbell Row

Bench-pressing heavy weights require stable shoulders and a strong back. And for that, it's important that all four muscles of your scapula are tight and strong.

Performing 3 to 5 sets of this exercise, with 8 to 12 reps each, will help you do that.

Banded Tricep Pushdowns

This is my favorite go-to for tricep accessories, as it can be set up virtually anywhere in the gym and gives a great pump when done correctly.

Simply attach an exercise band onto an overhead apparatus and push down on the edges of the band while pulling the two sides apart.

A common mistake that newer lifters make is that they don't take banded pushdowns seriously when doing them and perform the reps too fast without feeling out the tension.

Perform each rep in a slightly slower, more controlled manner and chase for a pump.

You can even do these one arm at a time for greater isolation in case you think one arm overpowers another. Perform 3 to 5 sets of 10 to 20 reps on this exercise.

If you can't fully extend downwards with the resistance being used, you are going too heavy.

Most lifters will either end up using a "mini" red band or "monster mini" black band for tricep pushdowns.

Accessory Movements for the Deadlift

Kettlebell Swings

At the time of this writing, the deadlift is arguably my most stubborn competition lift to raise, and I have only pulled 633 in competition.

Though I have recently pulled 635 in the off-season, my progress is haunted due to getting stuck right above the knees with a max pull.

For those of us who have a sticking point right above the knees until lock out with the deadlift, kettlebell swings can help when done with proper form.

This exercise helps strengthen the glutes, hamstrings, and abs while aiding towards loosening the hips.

For myself and a fair majority of lifters, my posterior chain is relatively weak compared to everything else and my hip mobility could always be improved.

You can use kettlebell swings right after a second barbell movement of either your Max Effort or Dynamic Effort session, or you can even incorporate them as part of your warm-up routine prior to any lower body workout.

The Lower-Trap Raise

One of the most taken for granted muscles, when it comes to performing deadlifts, are the lower-trapezius muscles, also known as trap-3. Strong trap-3 muscles help you keep your mid-back straight and ribcage raised while pulling on the deadlift.

This position allows you to deadlift optimal or maximum weights and reduces your risks for injury. To perform:

> Stand in front of an adjustable bench inclined at 90 degrees (perpendicular to the floor) or a fixed column or vertical bar.
>
> Holding a dumbbell with your right hand, bend at the waist – keep your lower back straight and legs slightly bent at all times – and brace your self on the bench or column with your left hand.
>
> Keeping your upper body inclined at a 45-degree angle, lift the barbell as high as you can before bringing down to the original position in a controlled manner.
>
> Keep your arms almost straight – with only a slight bend at the elbows to relieve it of excessive strain – all throughout the movement.
>
> Repeat the same for the left hand and perform 2 to 4 sets of 8 to 12 reps each per side.

Bridge (Hip Thrusts) – Barbell Version

Many lifters think that deadlifts are all about the lower back and hamstring muscles only. It's not.

The pelvic muscle is another crucial muscle for successfully deadlifting heavy weights, particularly at the latter part of the positive or concentric phase of the lift.

This exercise will help you strengthen and improve your ability to control your pelvic muscles for optimal deadlifting. To perform:

Begin by lying beneath a loaded barbell, with your pelvis directly beneath it. If you can't fit beneath it, consider placing it above two boxes for elevation.

Grip both sides of the barbell with your hands and plant your feet on the floor as close to your butt as possible by bending at the knees.

Lift the barbell with your pelvis until your body from the head to your knees forms a straight decline.

Keeping the barbell balanced and in place by maintaining a strong grip on both sides of the barbell, and applying just enough resistance to prevent it from sliding down to your upper body.

Bring the barbell down to starting position in a controlled manner. Perform 3 to 4 sets of 10 to 15 reps each.

JACOB ROTHENBERG

6. FINE TUNING CONJUGATE FOR RAW LIFTING

If you have ever turned to social media and internet message boards about powerlifting, you've surely encountered negative feedback & criticism about the conjugate method – moreover, the "Westside Conjugate System" is what gets bashed on.

A lot of people in this day & age still think that Westside Conjugate is in fact the Conjugate System in of itself, and that is where the problem lies therein.

While it can be tempting to get sensitive about the topic about retort with personal attacks, the truth is that Westside Conjugate has its flaws for powerlifters solely pursuing raw strength.

Chad Wesley Smith is among one of the smartest coaches around in this current era of powerlifting, and he is especially critical of Westside Conjugate for a number of valid reasons.

Though some of these points have already been previously mentioned in this book, here are CWS's critiques of Westside Conjugate:

- Most primary and secondary barbell movements emphasize on employing a partial range of motion. This does not carry over too well for raw lifting past a certain degree of strength, especially when one's sticking point is at the bottom of the lift.

  And for the majority of raw lifters squatting or benching, the lift's sticking point is going to be at the bottom portion of the lift – not the top.

- Westside does not prioritize training the deltoids and pectoral muscles as much as is necessary for a raw lifter to become strong at bench pressing, while staying healthy.

  While strong triceps and a strong back are vital components of a big bench, delts and pecs play an important role for not only pressing, but stabilization and control of the weight in motion.

- Westside is notorious for always squatting to a box in training with hardly any exception. This works great for geared lifting, where a suit will allow you to sit back into the material and put you in a position where you will get kinetic rebound from it.

Furthermore, box squats reinforce proper technique for geared powerlifting. While box squatting is a great tool for beginners to learn the basic mechanics of a squat, incorporating it as a mainstay of your program does not carry over for raw squatting.

Can you name a big time raw squatter who absolutely swears by the box squat? Probably not.

- There is a neglected aspect of training the quadriceps in Westside Conjugate. Due to being able to use a very wide stance while using a multi-ply suit, the primary movers are the hamstrings, glutes, hips, and posterior chain in a geared squat.

  For raw squatting, this same wide stance is not optimal for the majority of lifters. As such, a narrower stance employs the use of the quadriceps, which Westside Conjugate does not program exercises in particular to primarily target.

  If you want to be a good raw squatter, you need to have strong quads.

- The overload principles used in Westside lack a significant amount of volume necessary to develop overall muscle mass.

While the "typical" cookie cutter template designed to emulate Westside conjugate can develop muscle mass a novice level, there is simply not enough volume necessary to further develop an athlete to a more advanced level of possessing muscle mass.

As such, Westside needs a minimum volume threshold set for newer lifters who are not necessarily the same men at Westside Barbell who started relatively big with developed physiques from the beginning.

- Dynamic Effort work done in the "typical" template of 8-10 sets for main movements is still not enough volume necessary to build muscle mass, despite its intentions of providing more volume in conjunction with Max Effort.

- There is an increased injury occurrence and mental burnout with solely max singles using max effort.

- LACK OF SPECIFICITY! Westside Conjugate's biggest weakness for raw lifting is that the lack of overall specificity with prescribed movements.

All the fancy barbell movements and variations with boxes simply do not carry over for raw lifting. Imagine having to do a safety squat bar performed on a 15" box versus average bands and 80 pounds of chain for a max single and coming up with the rationale of how choosing exercises such as this will benefit your raw squat in the long term.

You need to be lifting actual weight on the bar, and rotate in movements that more closely resemble the competition lift – such as a close grip bench press, a deadlift for a max single while standing on top of a 2" deficit, a close stance high bar squat done for a max triple, and so forth.

- With exception to the deadlift, accommodating resistance does not have optimal applications for raw lifters.

    Similar to how utilizing a partial range of motion for the majority of your barbell movements will backfire, over-relying on bands and chains week in and week out will not do a whole lot for your competition lifts.

    Again, if you're stuck at the bottom portion of your press but you're the king of board presses, you're only fooling yourself into thinking you'll have a good bench pressing performance at your next meet.

- PRs on movement variations do not directly assess current abilities on competition lifts. To give you a very real example, I used to believe that my 2 board press had a 20 pound correlation to my competition bench press.

  So if I could 2 board 405 pounds, I would translate this into being able to press 385 pounds in competition. Well, it didn't work out like that for me when I tried pressing 385 at the 2013 IPL Worlds – all I could muster was a 369 pound press. Movement variations are just that – variations!

  Nothing will correctly assess your competition lift like actually performing the lift itself.

- There lack is of phase potentiation present in Westside Conjugate. While "phase potentiation" sounds like fancy scientific jargon, it simply refers to the training blocks that usually make up a strength program.

  These phases are categorized by most programs as Hypertrophy, Strength, Peaking, and Tapering.

  While this subject could be explained to the length of another book, Westside's periodization does not shift between hypertrophy or strength phases; at best, it utilizes a "Circa Max" wave for peaking multi-ply lifters.

> A raw powerlifter needs the specific phases of training blocks to optimize long term development of muscle mass, overall strength, and ability to overreach for meets.

Quite the list of everything flawed with Westside conjugate, isn't it?

Fortunately, a lot of these issues have been mitigated with the programming designed by my coach, Jesse Burdick with his methodology of conjugate.

Here are some of the adjustments we have made with using conjugate to better suit a raw lifter.

These are the actual notes that I originally published online as my very first article for powerlifting, and they are still 100% valid today.

1. We emphasize working on sticking points that are more related to a raw lifter's weaknesses.

    You can get very strong at pressing off of 3 boards if you constantly do it, but chances are your raw bench won't improve at all if you're always getting stuck off your chest. You have to be logical with your movement selections and accessory work. Instead of doing 3 board versus mini bands for your Max Effort movement, try benching using the Duffalo/Buffalo bar for a 5 rep max if you need to be stronger at the bottom of the lift.

While it is completely appropriate (and necessary) to use overload methods in your training, try to utilize more movements that specifically key your weak point(s).

2. To parlay what I just said about benching, we don't always lift to a 1 rep max on Max Effort days. Program ME days that call for lifting to a 3-5 rep max.

   Yes, this directly contradicts Louie's notion about Max Effort - he'll tell you that Max Effort is exclusively pertaining to max singles.

   That being said, myself and others have found that the occurrence of injury is reduced when you're not lifting to a 1 rep max every week, and it is also easier to recover when you're not trying to blow your brains to the wall every single session.

   If I am not mistaken, Brandon Lilly's premise for the Cube Method was that lifting to max singles wasn't always necessary every week and it was for the same reasons mentioned.

   Also, if you look at most of the top raw lifters of this era, they tend to mix in 3-5 RM work on their heavy days.

3. We use a LOT more volume on our Dynamic Effort days. When I first joined Jesse's gym, I thought he was nuts when I saw on the board that

he typically programs sets of 12-20 for DE bench. And don't get me started on DE lower -- we're often doing 15-20 sets of squats AND 8-10 sets of deadlifting on the same day. After four years of doing the typical 8 sets of bench and 8 sets of squat for "speed work", this took a lot of adjusting to and I still have a tough time completing all the work even up to now.

All that said, one of the main criticisms of using Westside as a raw lifter is that there isn't enough volume for significant strength (or size) gains to be made.

This is completely true if you're thinking that squatting 225 for 8 sets of 2 for DE every week will make you a 600 lb squatter....chances are it won't.

As a starting guideline, I'd recommend doubling your current volume for DE movements along with squatting AND deadlifting on the same day for DE every week.

4. Another criticism of Westside for raw lifters is that there is not enough specificity in the barbell movements to properly prepare (or "peak") a powerlifter for meet day.

I agree with this, on the notion that the use of contrast (bands, chains, etc.) throws off the natural groove of a barbell movement and the dynamics of how the weight is moved change as opposed to just lifting a regular barbell with "straight weight" (no contrast).

While we still do plenty of specialized movements for the lifts throughout a training cycle, we switch back to doing the classical lifts 6-7 weeks out from a meet.

You need to be technically skilled at the lifts, and being prepared on competition day means having practiced the 3 lifts enough to not give any error to a big technique/form flaw during your meet.

5. We do not squat to a box on every DE lower day.

6. We don't always use contrast on DE day for any of the lifts. More often than not we actually bench & squat with straight weight.

7. We don't skimp out on accessory work. Along with getting volume in with the compound movements, we also regularly perform 3-5 accessory movements on each day.

Not only are you addressing weak points with accessories, but you are also trying to build the muscle mass necessary to progress as a lifter. Muscle moves weight, people!

When was the last time you saw a 150 lb kid bench 405 raw? Unless you're in the presence of a genetic freak, it just doesn't happen and you need to look like you lift weights if you want to move bigger weights.

JACOB ROTHENBERG

8. PUTTING IT TOGETHER

As we end this book, I want you to get a clearer picture of how you can implement the raw conjugate method of powerlifting for achieving overall objectives of gaining strength, power and speed necessary to make gains in your lifts.

Here is a sample 1 week template of how my own split looks like for conjugate training.

It's worth noting that in order for optimal training sessions, you must be able to lift 4 days a week to set up the conjugate system. You can even throw in a 5th day for extra back work along with any supplementary accessory work you want to add in to target weaknesses, provided that you give yourself the recovery capacity to do such.

Monday (Max Effort Lower)

1. Warm ups for 10 minutes. My personal warm-up includes mobility/stretch drills for my hips and

lower back – this includes static stretching, walking a couple laps outside the gym using Mark Bell's hip circle, and foam rolling.

2. Squats with the Safety Squat Bar (SSB) for a max triple. After a max triple is reached, drop set down to 80% of weight used for 2 AMRAP sets (as many reps as possible).

3. Romanian deadlifts for 3 sets of 15 using a light weight. I use straps on these if my holding grip gets shot throughout the sets.

4. Glute-ham raises off the GHR machine for 3 sets of 10 reps each.

5. Reverse Hyperextensions for 4 sets of 8 to 12 reps each.

6. Roman Chair Sit Ups off the GHR machine weights for 5 sets of 10 reps each.

Wednesday (Max Effort Upper)

1. Warm ups for 5 minutes. For myself, this includes standard mobility & stretch drills using bands along with very light overhead dumbbell presses.

   Regardless of what max effort bench movement I have to do, I take an empty bar and press it for 20 reps, then take 135 & 185 for a few reps before cutting down to triples with 225 to warm up.

2. Bench Press versus 80 pounds of chain for a max

single (refer to the Max Effort chapter for guidelines on working up to your 1-rep max). After reaching a max single, drop set to 80% of weight reached and perform 2 AMRAP sets.

3. Close Grip Bench Press for 5 sets of 10-12 reps each.

4. Cable Lat Pulldowns for 5 sets of 8 to 12 reps each.

5. Barbell / Dumbbell Tricep Extension for 3 to 5 sets of 8 to 12 reps each.

6. Banded Tricep Pushdowns for 3 sets of 15 reps each.

7. Dumbbell Curls for 3-5 sets of 10 reps each.

Friday (Dynamic Effort Lower)

1. Warm ups for 10 minutes. My personal warm-up includes mobility/stretch drills for my hips and lower back – this includes static stretching, walking a couple laps outside the gym using Mark Bell's hip circle, and foam rolling.

2. Pause squats for 10 sets, using no accommodating resistance. First 5 sets are performed with 50% of your squat max for 3 reps each. Second series of 5 sets are performed with 60% of your squat max for 2 reps each.

3. Deadlifts for 10 sets of singles using 60% of your deadlift max, performed with "light" orange bands attached.

4. Dumbbell Step Ups for 3 sets of 15 reps each leg.

5. Banded Leg Curls for 3 sets, each set done for a 2 minute duration.

6. Ab Pulldowns for 3 sets of 10 reps each

Saturday (Dynamic Effort Upper)

1. Warm ups for 5 minutes. For myself, this includes standard mobility & stretch drills using bands along with very light overhead dumbbell presses.

   Regardless of what dynamic effort bench movement I have to do, I take an empty bar and press it for 20 reps, then take 135 for 5 reps before proceeding on with the remainder of my primary movement.

2. Bench Press for 10 to 12 sets of 3 reps each, performed with resistance bands or chains and fast movement.

3. Dumbbell Incline Presses for 2 to 4 sets of 8 to 12 reps each.

4. Barbell French Presses for 2 to 4 sets of 8 to 12 reps each.

5. Hammer Curls for 2 to 4 sets of 8 to 12 reps each.

General Guidelines

- Don't forget to warm up first!

  Even when you're starting out and relatively healthy with no existing training injuries, you want to warm up and stretch prior to any training session.

  Preventing injuries is one of the fundamental keys to becoming a strong powerlifter.

- Always prioritize movements with a full range of motion for your exercise selection on Max Effort days.

  This is essential for raw lifting due to lack of "assistance" from single/multi-ply equipment.

  You can occasionally rotate in 2 board / Manpon press work from time to time, but don't make it a staple of your primary movement selection.

- For strengthening your weak points when performing exercises within their full ranges of motion, it's important to incorporate at least 1 accessory exercise or movement related to it.

  For example, if you know your hamstrings are your sticking point in the squat, as you're unable to drive out of the hole in a max attempt – hit the GHR machine hard and consistently.

- Always let a minimum of 72 hours pass from your previous dynamic or max effort workouts prior to performing a max effort workout to ensure full recuperation.

- If you are entirely new to lifting, you can opt to change out your max effort exercise every 2-3 sessions instead of every week.

  For the base movements or lifts, use different variations of the same, i.e., regular grip bench press, close grip bench press, and medium grip bench press (between regular your and close grip).

  As you progress, you should change the exercises more frequently until you a more intermediate or advanced lifter, at which point you should change the primary movement every week.

- When reintroducing an exercise as your primary movement, wait for at least 8 weeks from the last time they were last performed before doing so.

CONCLUSION

Thank you for buying this book!

I hope it was able to help you learn much about the conjugate method for powerlifting, particularly for lifting raw. My objective was to provide a clearer understanding of how conjugate *should* be modified and applied for raw powerlifters, as I genuinely want to see the training method become more popular during this current era of the sport.

It is a fantastic training methodology when applied correctly, and there are still so many misconceptions about conjugate which prevent powerlifters from potentially learning about it.

This book is the first entry of a four-part series about the raw conjugate method. "Foundations" sets the general blueprint for programming the conjugate

system for raw lifting; the next three books will cover each competitive lift in much greater detail using conjugate.

I will eventually go over the finer details of programming & training each lift using conjugate, and cover just about everything you need to know as far as weak point training, all the special exercises to choose from, and so on.

Stay tuned and check back on Amazon every few weeks for the latest book of this series.

But more than just learning about the conjugate system, I want to encourage you to take immediate steps towards applying what you learned and set up your training program.

After all, knowing is only half the battle and the other half is action or application of knowledge.

The longer you put off applying what you learned here, the more likely it is you won't apply the concepts you've learned in this book at all.

Start now, and begin your path towards long-term success in your own powerlifting goals!

Here's to your powerlifting success my friend! Cheers!

ABOUT THE AUTHOR

Jacob Rothenberg is a powerlifter with current best competition lifts of a 633 lb. squat, 418 lb. bench, and 633 lb. deadlift in the 242 lb. weight division.

Having started from very humble beginnings of totaling 1,000 pounds in his first powerlifting meet, Jacob has dedicated over 8 years towards competitive powerlifting & learning from the best coaches in the world about the "conjugate" training system.

He hopes to achieve further success on the platform while also enabling newer lifters towards reaching their fullest potential by means of sharing information & knowledge through his written works.

Outside of powerlifting, Jacob works as an international sales manager for a construction & mechanical supply company in the California Bay Area.

Having started college at the age of 11, he graduated from UC Davis with a Bachelor of Arts at 16 years old and completed his MBA at the age of 23.

His interests include reading, traveling to new destinations, learning different cultures and trying local cuisine.

Made in the USA
Monee, IL
15 December 2021